This book was donated through the...

Ben Carson Reading Room Grant

March 1, 2004

MAPS & MAPMAKERS

MAPS & MAPMAKERS

Maps in Everyday Life

Martyn Bramwell

Illustrated by George Fryer

Lerner Publications Company • Minneapolis

This edition published in 1998

Lerner Publications Company
241 First Avenue North
Minneapolis MN 55401

Printed in Italy by Vallardi Industrie Grafich s.p.a.
Bound in the United States of America

Library of Congress Cataloging-in-Publication Data

Bramwell, Martyn.
     Maps in everyday life / by Martyn Bramwell.
        p.   cm. – (Maps & mapmakers)
     Includes references and index.
     Summary: Describes many different kinds of maps used in daily life including weather, road, and street maps as well as those showing specialized information and even mall directories.
     ISBN 0-8225-2923-8 (lib. bdg. : alk. paper)
     1. Maps–Juvenile literature. [1. Maps.] I. Title.
II. Series: Bramwell, Martyn. Maps & mapmakers.
GA130.B645   1998
912–dc21   97-27282

Acknowledgments

Thanks to Old Sturbridge Village for providing the map and pictures on page 12, Streetwise Maps for the use of the Artwise map on pages 14-15, Hubbard Scientific/Scott Resources for the picture on page 16, Foster and Partners for the picture on page 17, Mall of America for the pictures on pages 30-31 and page 39, Microsoft for the pictures on pages 42-43, and Oldsmobile for the pictures on pages 44-45.

Contents

UNDERGROUND

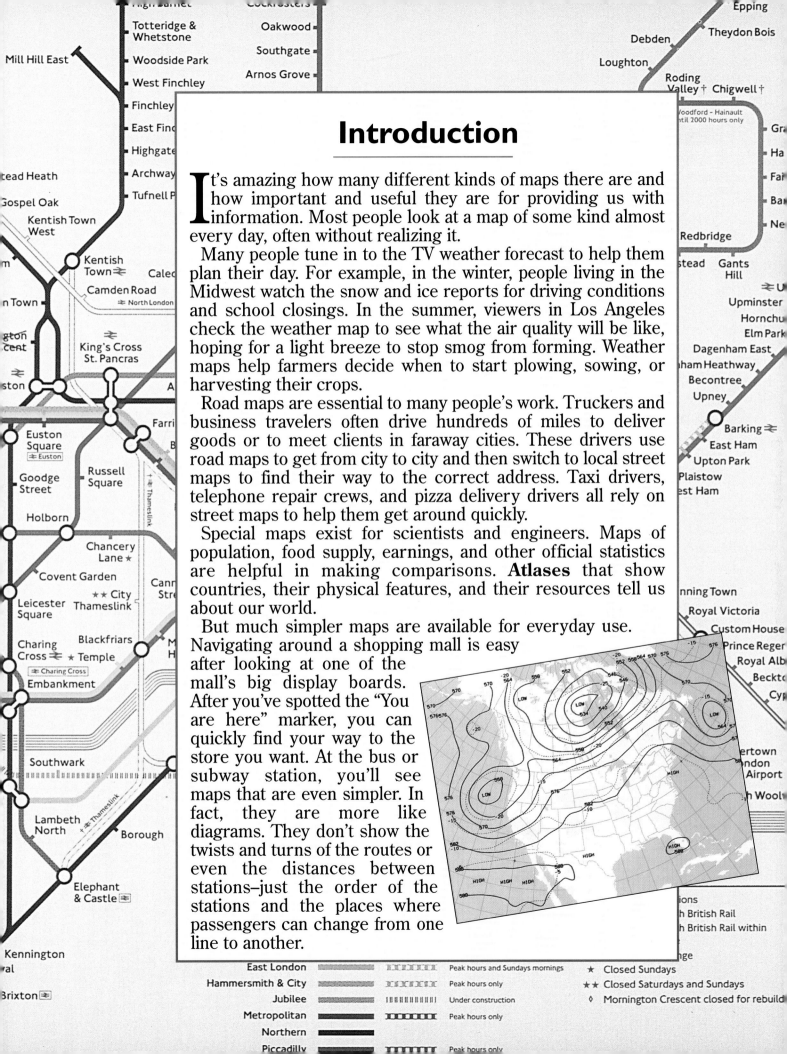

Introduction

It's amazing how many different kinds of maps there are and how important and useful they are for providing us with information. Most people look at a map of some kind almost every day, often without realizing it.

Many people tune in to the TV weather forecast to help them plan their day. For example, in the winter, people living in the Midwest watch the snow and ice reports for driving conditions and school closings. In the summer, viewers in Los Angeles check the weather map to see what the air quality will be like, hoping for a light breeze to stop smog from forming. Weather maps help farmers decide when to start plowing, sowing, or harvesting their crops.

Road maps are essential to many people's work. Truckers and business travelers often drive hundreds of miles to deliver goods or to meet clients in faraway cities. These drivers use road maps to get from city to city and then switch to local street maps to find their way to the correct address. Taxi drivers, telephone repair crews, and pizza delivery drivers all rely on street maps to help them get around quickly.

Special maps exist for scientists and engineers. Maps of population, food supply, earnings, and other official statistics are helpful in making comparisons. **Atlases** that show countries, their physical features, and their resources tell us about our world.

But much simpler maps are available for everyday use. Navigating around a shopping mall is easy after looking at one of the mall's big display boards. After you've spotted the "You are here" marker, you can quickly find your way to the store you want. At the bus or subway station, you'll see maps that are even simpler. In fact, they are more like diagrams. They don't show the twists and turns of the routes or even the distances between stations–just the order of the stations and the places where passengers can change from one line to another.

Landscape Maps

Maps that provide us with a detailed picture of the landscape are called **topographical** or **physical maps**. They show the natural shape, or relief, of the land surface with all its hills and valleys, plains and sea cliffs. They also mark locations of towns, cities, roads, railroads, bridges, dams, and harbors.

Of all the different types of maps, topographical maps provide the best overall view of the landscape. **Contour lines**, colors, and hill shading represent the shape of the land surface. Contour lines are fine lines joining places that are the same height above sea level. An oval-shaped hill, for example, is shown by a series of oval lines, one inside the other. The lines have numbers on them, noting their height above sea level. The ovals get smaller toward the top of the hill. The smallest oval, in the middle of the group, will have the highest number, indicating the hilltop.

V-shaped patterns of lines represent valleys (if the highest numbers are on the outside of the V) or narrow mountain ridges (if the highest numbers are on the inside). Widely spaced lines indicate gentle slopes, while tightly packed lines show very steep slopes.

Many maps use colors to represent land at various heights, and the best maps also apply shading to create an impression of shadows cast by high ground. Lines of different colors and thicknesses mark roads and railroads. Symbols indicate different types of vegetation, such as forest and grassland, and also

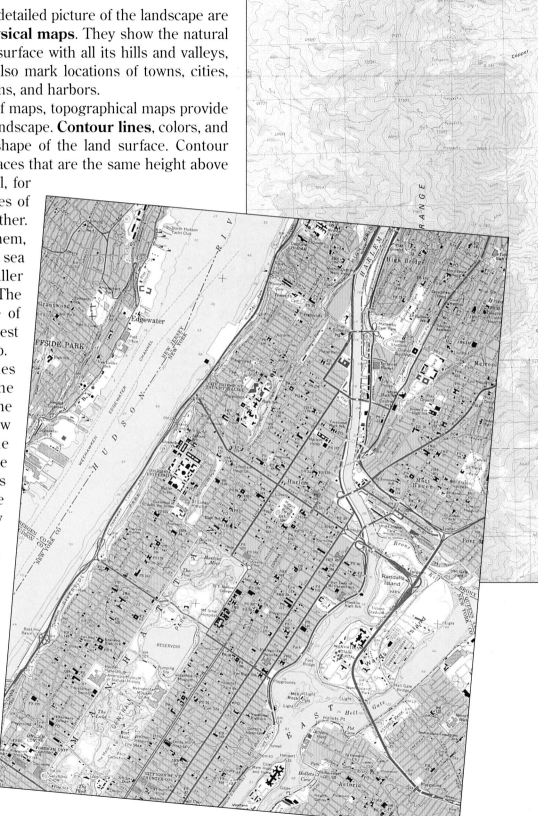

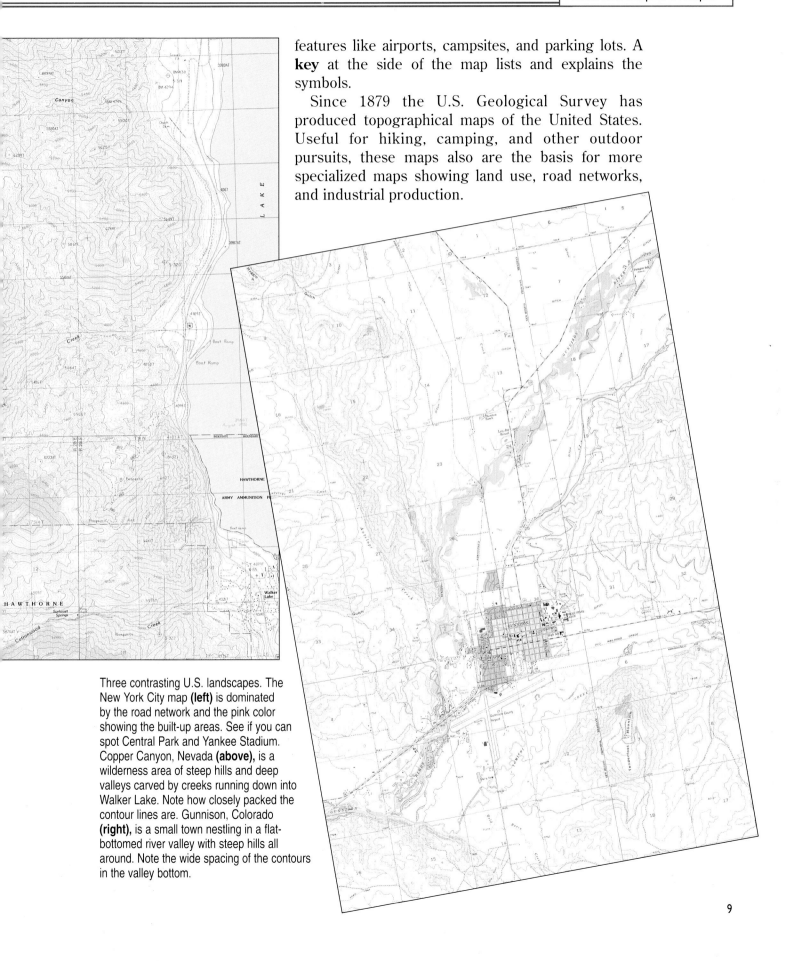

features like airports, campsites, and parking lots. A **key** at the side of the map lists and explains the symbols.

Since 1879 the U.S. Geological Survey has produced topographical maps of the United States. Useful for hiking, camping, and other outdoor pursuits, these maps also are the basis for more specialized maps showing land use, road networks, and industrial production.

Three contrasting U.S. landscapes. The New York City map **(left)** is dominated by the road network and the pink color showing the built-up areas. See if you can spot Central Park and Yankee Stadium. Copper Canyon, Nevada **(above),** is a wilderness area of steep hills and deep valleys carved by creeks running down into Walker Lake. Note how closely packed the contour lines are. Gunnison, Colorado **(right),** is a small town nestling in a flat-bottomed river valley with steep hills all around. Note the wide spacing of the contours in the valley bottom.

Road Maps

Travelers use road maps to find the best route from one place to another. A business traveler looking for the quickest and most direct route might use a road map to locate interstate highways and other main roads. A tourist's best route might be the most scenic one or one that takes in several interesting towns or historic sites. Vacationers are more likely to travel on secondary roads to explore the country at a more leisurely pace.

Cartographers (people who create maps) draw road maps at many different **scales** to accommodate different needs. (The scale of a map is a measure of how many miles on the ground are represented by each inch on the map.) A business traveler planning a journey from Michigan to Florida or a tourist setting up a vacation across the United States from Georgia to California might start with a small-scale map–one that shows a large area although not in great detail. These travelers might use a map with a scale of about 90 miles to the inch, which would show most of the United States on a single fold-out sheet measuring 36 x 24 inches.

Road atlases scaled at 20 or 30 miles to the inch are ideal for detailed route planning. These atlases usually have large pages and cover a whole state at a time, showing the secondary roads and small towns as well as highways and main cities. Many road atlases also include street maps of the main cities, maps of state and national parks, and special scenic routes.

Large-scale maps provide even more detail. A highway atlas for a single state, for example, might contain maps at a scale of 3 miles to 1 inch. At this scale the maps will show all the rest areas, historic sites, covered bridges, famous buildings, and sports facilities like golf courses, marinas, ski resorts, beaches, campsites, nature trails, and visitor centers. State road atlases also often include diagrams of the most complicated highway interchanges to help drivers take the correct exit.

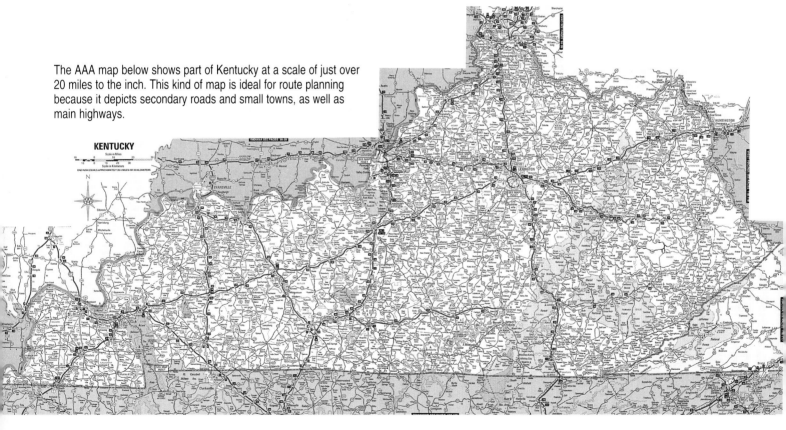

The AAA map below shows part of Kentucky at a scale of just over 20 miles to the inch. This kind of map is ideal for route planning because it depicts secondary roads and small towns, as well as main highways.

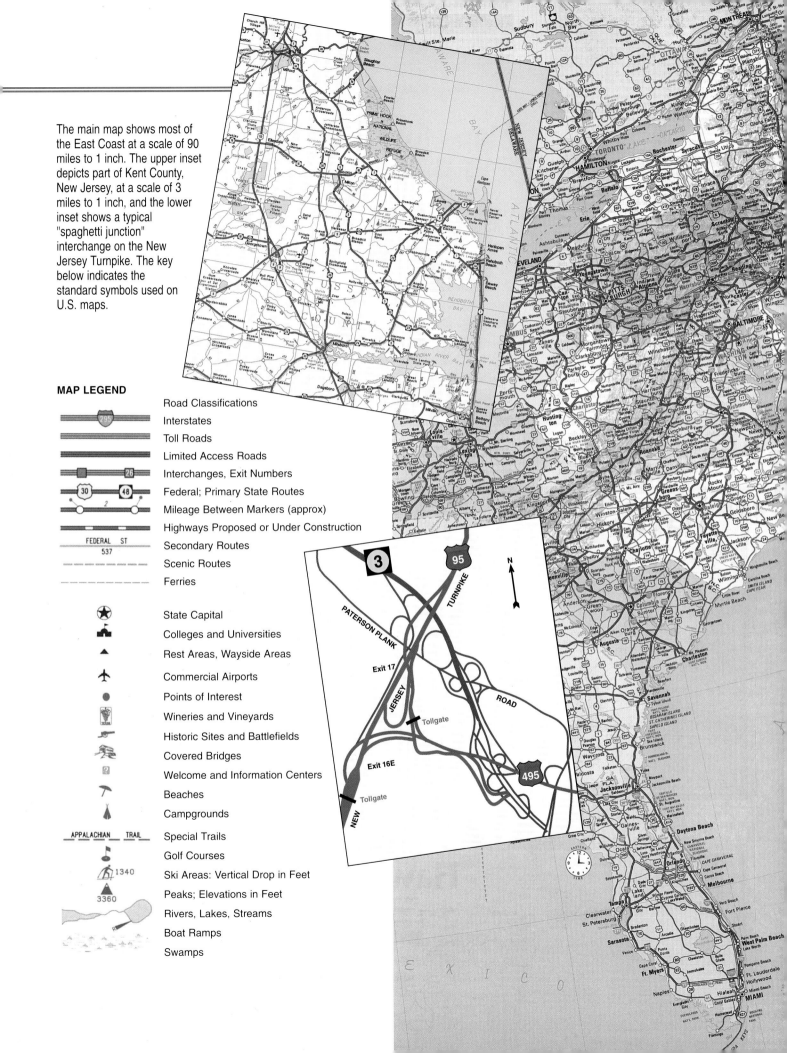

The main map shows most of the East Coast at a scale of 90 miles to 1 inch. The upper inset depicts part of Kent County, New Jersey, at a scale of 3 miles to 1 inch, and the lower inset shows a typical "spaghetti junction" interchange on the New Jersey Turnpike. The key below indicates the standard symbols used on U.S. maps.

MAP LEGEND

Road Classifications

Interstates

Toll Roads

Limited Access Roads

Interchanges, Exit Numbers

Federal; Primary State Routes

Mileage Between Markers (approx)

Highways Proposed or Under Construction

FEDERAL ST
537

Secondary Routes

Scenic Routes

Ferries

State Capital

Colleges and Universities

Rest Areas, Wayside Areas

Commercial Airports

Points of Interest

Wineries and Vineyards

Historic Sites and Battlefields

Covered Bridges

Welcome and Information Centers

Beaches

Campgrounds

APPALACHIAN TRAIL Special Trails

Golf Courses

1340 Ski Areas: Vertical Drop in Feet

3360 Peaks; Elevations in Feet

Rivers, Lakes, Streams

Boat Ramps

Swamps

Maps for Tourists and Backpackers

The first step in producing a map is called the compilation stage, and the **compiler**–the person who collects all the information that will go on the map–first has to answer some very important questions. "Who is this map for?" "What information do they need?" "What is the clearest way of showing that information?"

If vacationers are to use the map, the compiler will combine several different kinds of information. The map has to indicate the area's main roads, but it must also include minor roads for leisurely exploration. In hilly country, paved roads must be distinguished from rough tracks. Maps of mountainous regions might need labels warning of road closures. Maps of desert regions could explain the dangers of wandering off the highway.

Along with roads, tourist maps will indicate footpaths. Some of the paths are recommended routes across open country that backpackers and hikers can use. Others are nature trails or historical walks that loop from a visitor center, where there are shops, restaurants, restrooms, and other facilities. These trails often include picnic sites, and viewpoints with descriptions of unusual rock formations, wildlife, and other features.

Historic buildings, battlefields, craft centers, museums, and art galleries remain popular vacation stops. The compiler will mark these features with symbols, and, if space allows, may note hours of operation and entrance fees.

For backpackers carrying tents or vacationers in campers and trailers, the map will show symbols for campsites and trailer parks. For people who like sports activities, symbols will tell the map user where to go skiing, wind surfing, climbing, or sailing.

One of the most exciting ways of exploring your country's history is by visiting a "living museum" like the one at Old Sturbridge in Massachusetts. Here, rural New England in the 1830s is vividly brought to life throughout the year. Staff in period costume demonstrate the way of life, work, crafts, and customs of the early nineteenth century, against a backdrop of carefully restored buildings and artifacts.

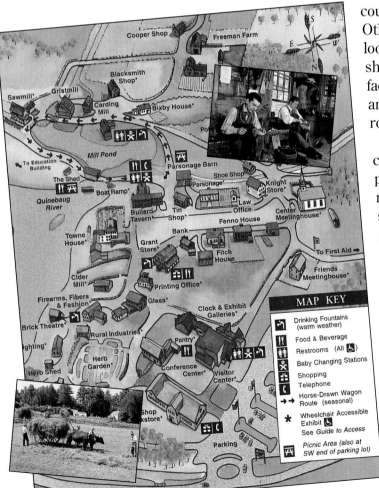

Right: Yellowstone National Park in Wyoming, founded in 1872, was the world's first national park and is still one of the most popular tourist destinations. The park has geysers and waterfalls, towering rock faces, silent lakes, and a wealth of wildlife. Yellowstone can be explored by car and on foot in summer and by ski or snowmobile in winter.

Street Maps and City Guides

Visit the travel section of any large bookstore and you will find hundreds of city maps–either as single, large fold-out maps or in guidebooks. The maps are divided into grid squares that are further identified by letters along the top of the map and numbers down the side (or the other way around). Usually an index–a list of street names–is included, and next to each street name is the code for the grid square in which the street can be found. The entry for a very long street may give grid square references for both ends, such as "Constitution Avenue B2-F8." Many tourist maps contain several indexes –one for street names, another for historic buildings, and still others for museums, hotels, theaters, restaurants, and other places of interest.

City maps come in many different styles. Some are simple black-and-white street maps. Others color code bus and subway routes and identify taxi stops, public telephones, museums, and theaters with easily recognized symbols. Some of the most decorative maps start with a simple street map and add small three-dimensional drawings of sites of local interest, each in its actual location.

City guidebooks provide even more information. Most start with a short description of the city's history, followed

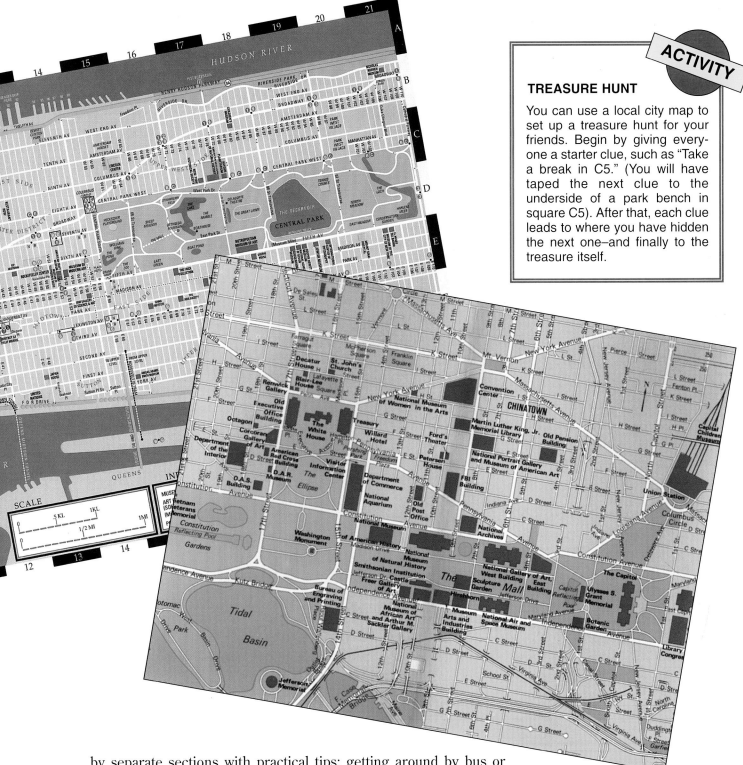

by separate sections with practical tips: getting around by bus or subway, finding museums with the latest interactive exhibits, locating the best hot dog stand, or where the most affordable shops are. Many city guidebooks also print the dates of festivals, parades, and major sporting events. You'll even find information on places of interest outside the city limits.

Tabletop Maps

A tabletop relief map is a three-dimensional (3-D) model of part of the earth's surface. It is usually set a few feet off the ground so people can walk around it and view it from all sides. The designer chooses the model's size and scale after determining the features and the area of ground the model is to represent.

Architects often use scale models to display their plans for big projects like airports, harbors, shopping malls, and parks. The models allow everyone to see what the new buildings will look like and how they will fit in among existing buildings and the surrounding landscape.

Landscape architects and designers often use 3-D models outdoors to explain the layout of large areas such as national parks, nature reserves, or historic battlefield sites. These models are usually sealed inside weatherproof glass or plastic cases and are placed at high viewpoints so visitors can match the features they see in the real landscape with the labeled features on the model. Resorts often display 3-D models so their guests can view the layouts of footpaths, nature trails, mountain-bike trails, and ski runs.

Companies choose many different materials to make landscape and architectural models, including balsa wood, plastic, cardboard, clay, plaster, and papier-mâché. Usually only one of each 3-D map is required. However, some companies also create 3-D relief maps for use in schools. These maps have to be produced in large numbers, exactly the same every time. Plastic relief maps are created by first printing the map on a flat sheet of vinyl (a type of plastic). The printed sheet is then shaped over a 3-D mold of the landscape cut from a solid block of aluminum or epoxy. The vinyl is heated to 752° F while it is on the mold, and when it cools it keeps its new 3-D shape.

Plastic relief maps are a great help in studying geography. Sighted students can see the shape of the land at a glance, and students with limited vision can explore the map by touch.

Plastic relief maps like this one of the Rocky Mountains can be placed flat on a table or mounted on the wall. They are especially useful for portraying the physical shape of mountain ranges and volcanic islands such as Hawaii.

An architect's model of a large urban development allows city planners and members of the public to see what the new buildings will look like and what impact they will have upon their surroundings. In this way, people's opinions can be heard before the project goes ahead.

Make a Relief Model

You can make a 3-D map from leftover household materials. Start with a wooden base. Then build up supports for the areas of high ground using clean food and drink containers. Tack a length of chicken wire to one edge of the base and then bend it over the supports and press it down into the shape you want. Cover the chicken wire with papier-mâché and allow it to dry. Finish the map by painting on the roads, towns, and vegetation, or turn it into a model by sticking on moss (woodland), a mirror (lake), small wooden blocks (buildings) and so on.

ACTIVITY

Vegetation and Land-use Maps

People in hundreds of different jobs need maps showing information about what lies on, under, or above the surface of the earth. These maps cover topics as varied as natural vegetation, climate, soil types, population, what crops are grown where, what minerals lie under the surface, and how much water is in the rivers. Maps of this type are called **thematic maps**, because each one deals with a particular theme, or topic. Teachers, weather forecasters, civil engineers, farmers, economists, government planners, and other professionals rely on thematic maps to do their jobs.

One of the most common thematic maps, a **vegetation map**, shows an area's natural vegetation (also called its potential vegetation). These tell us the types of vegetation that would cover the land if people had not cut down forests or plowed grasslands.

Below: Only about 11 percent of the world's land area is set aside for farming. Most of the land is too hot, too dry, too wet, or too cold. Another problem is that some areas have more food than they need, while people in other areas are permanently hungry. North America has about 8 percent of the world's population but 20 percent of the food supply. At the other extreme, Africa has 10 percent of the population but only 4 percent of the food supply, and Asia is even worse off with 40 percent of the world's people trying to survive on just 14 percent of the food supply.

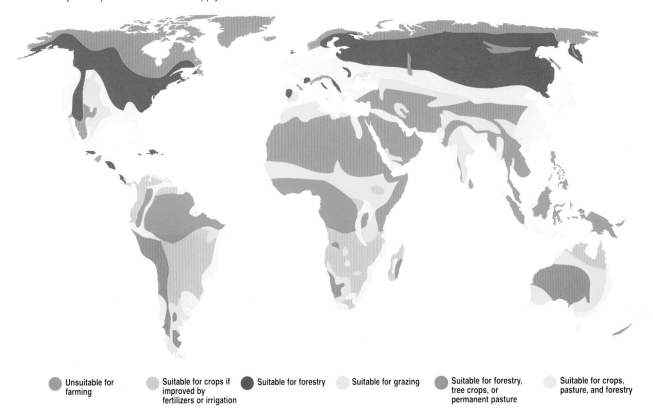

- Unsuitable for farming
- Suitable for crops if improved by fertilizers or irrigation
- Suitable for forestry
- Suitable for grazing
- Suitable for forestry, tree crops, or permanent pasture
- Suitable for crops, pasture, and forestry

Vegetation maps usually have a simple color key. On more detailed maps, small key letters or numbers can be printed on each color area to provide extra information.

Land-use maps give a more accurate picture because they show developed land as well as natural areas. A typical land-use map will indicate irrigated land, cropland, grazing land, farmland where both crops and animals are raised, and areas where farming mixes with untouched forest or grassland. The map will also show areas of untouched forest, grassland, and marsh as well as built-up residential, commercial, and industrial areas.

Left: Maps are a helpful way of comparing one country with another. These young people are learning about land use in different countries by looking at the thematic maps in an atlas.

Below: This map shows the "potential vegetation" of the United States–that is, the vegetation that would still cover the land if there were no farms, mines, cities, and road networks.

- Redwood forest
- Dry pine forest
- Dry scrub and steppes
- Coniferous forest
- Swamp
- Swamp forest
- Tree and shrub savanna
- Prairie grasslands
- Mixed deciduous forest
- Mountain forest
- Mixed evergreen forest

Geology Maps

With colors and symbols, geological maps show the three families of rocks that make up the earth's surface. **Igneous rocks** begin forming deep inside the earth as molten magma. The igneous group includes granite, which cools and hardens below the earth's surface, and various kinds of lava that pour out of volcanoes. **Sedimentary rocks** like sandstone make up the second family. They are composed of tiny fragments of other rocks worn down by wind, rain, rivers, and glaciers. The tiny rock fragments filter into the oceans and settle on the bottom in layers called beds or strata. Limestones, consisting of the shells of tiny sea creatures, form in the same way. Over millions of years, movements of the earth's crust can crumple these rock layers into folds, and push them thousands of feet above sea level.

The third family, called **metamorphic rocks**, are old rocks that have been altered by heat and pressure. The most familiar metamorphic rocks are marble, which was originally limestone, and slate, which began as mudstone.

Geologists (people who study the earth's rocks) make maps by identifying rock types and marking them on a base map. These scientists collect samples of rock and examine them later in a laboratory. If the rocks are layered, the geologist measures the slope of the beds with a **clinometer**. This instrument allows the geologist to determine if the layers have been squeezed into folds or broken along huge cracks called faults. The shapes that the rock layers make are called geological structures.

Left and below: These illustrations depict a geology map just as the geologist drew it. The boundaries of the different rock types are marked, along with the slope (dip) of the beds. Lines A-A and B-B highlight the position of the two cross sections shown below. The West-East section tells us that the rocks have been folded and faulted.

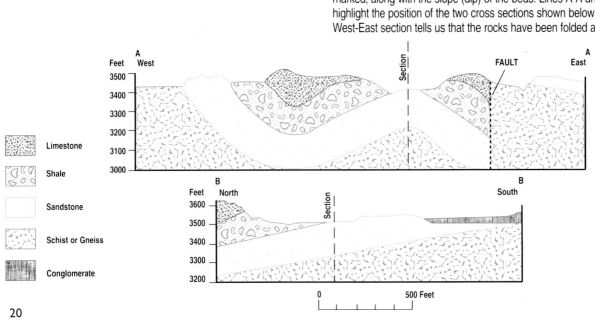

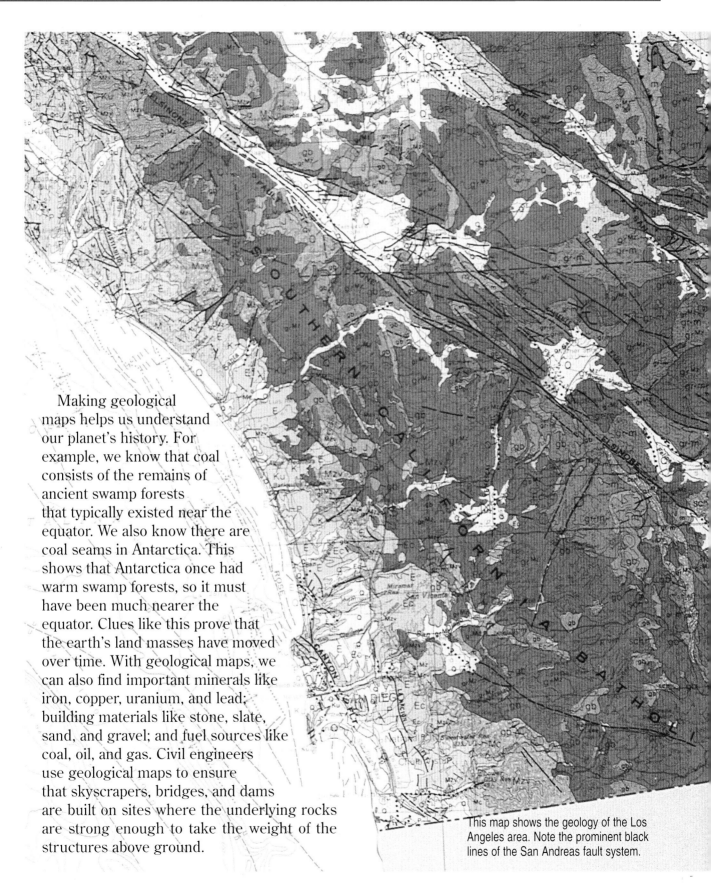

Making geological maps helps us understand our planet's history. For example, we know that coal consists of the remains of ancient swamp forests that typically existed near the equator. We also know there are coal seams in Antarctica. This shows that Antarctica once had warm swamp forests, so it must have been much nearer the equator. Clues like this prove that the earth's land masses have moved over time. With geological maps, we can also find important minerals like iron, copper, uranium, and lead; building materials like stone, slate, sand, and gravel; and fuel sources like coal, oil, and gas. Civil engineers use geological maps to ensure that skyscrapers, bridges, and dams are built on sites where the underlying rocks are strong enough to take the weight of the structures above ground.

This map shows the geology of the Los Angeles area. Note the prominent black lines of the San Andreas fault system.

21

Weather and Climate Maps

Although closely related, weather and climate are distinct features. Weather is the atmospheric conditions at a particular place and time. It might be hot, humid, and calm one day; and cold, wet, and windy the next–or even later the same day. Climate, on the other hand, is the average of the local weather over a long period of time. Day-to-day changes are unimportant. It is the pattern of sunshine, rainfall, and temperature over an entire year that defines a climate.

Masses of air, driven by the sun's heat, move over the earth's surface and produce weather. Warm air rises and cold air falls. As the air masses swim around, they interact with one another and with the land and sea. The air masses transport heat and moisture from one part of the atmosphere to another. The rising and falling air masses also create areas of low and high air pressure, which control the strength and direction of the wind.

All air masses contain water vapor–an invisible gas. Air masses pick up the water vapor as they move over oceans, lakes, and land. Warm air can hold more water vapor than cold air, but when warm air is forced up by mountains or by riding over a mass of cold air, it gets cooler and some of its water vapor condenses–that is, it changes from a gas into microscopic water droplets. These tiny droplets form clouds. If conditions are right, the droplets combine into bigger drops and eventually fall as rain, sleet, hail, or snow.

Meteorologists (weather scientists) collect information every three hours from hundreds of local, national, and international weather stations. Each station reports the temperature, air pressure, visibility, wind speed and direction, humidity (the amount of water in the air), and the height and amount of cloud cover. The scientists plot this information on a chart and use it to forecast the weather. From this detailed information, meteorologists draw simplified maps for TV weather forecasts.

Right: This map shows how U.S. meteorologists plotted the weather information for North America on June 29, 1997. The pattern of high and low pressure enabled the scientists to predict wind speed and direction and how much sunshine or rain there would be.

Below: This map shows the world's main climate types. Look at the world maps of temperature, rainfall, and winds in an atlas and you will see how closely they tie in with the pattern of the climate zones.

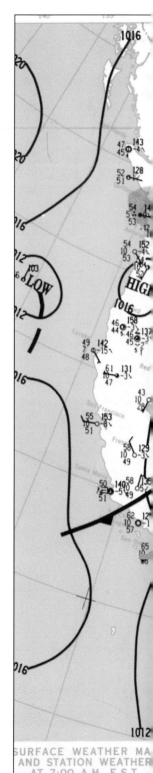

SURFACE WEATHER MA
AND STATION WEATHER
AT 7:00 A.M., E.S.T.

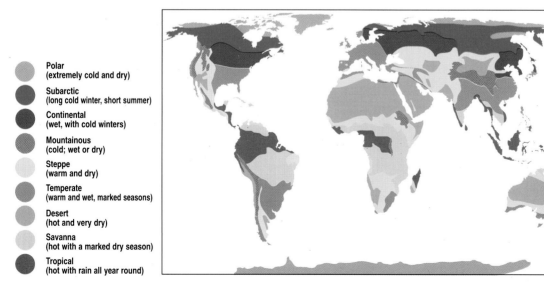

Polar
(extremely cold and dry)

Subarctic
(long cold winter, short summer)

Continental
(wet, with cold winters)

Mountainous
(cold; wet or dry)

Steppe
(warm and dry)

Temperate
(warm and wet, marked seasons)

Desert
(hot and very dry)

Savanna
(hot with a marked dry season)

Tropical
(hot with rain all year round)

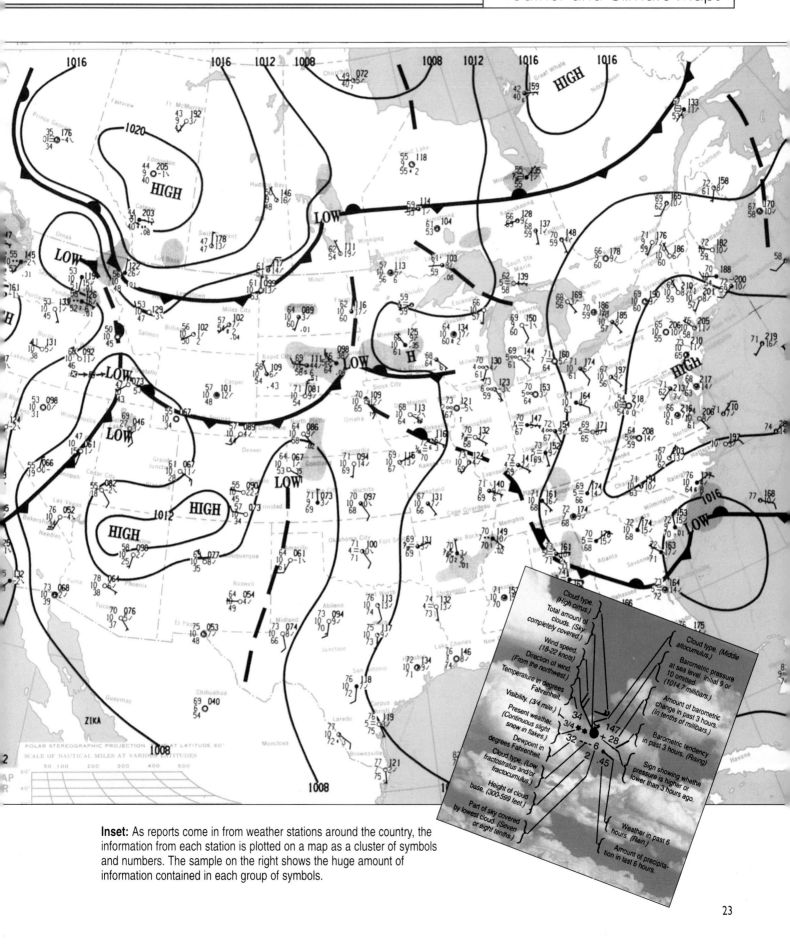

Inset: As reports come in from weather stations around the country, the information from each station is plotted on a map as a cluster of symbols and numbers. The sample on the right shows the huge amount of information contained in each group of symbols.

Dots, Symbols, and Colors

Cartographers can plot almost any information on a map provided the information can be expressed in numbers and the numbers vary across the region. These mapmakers convey the information using colors, symbols, or combinations of both to show distribution (where a particular thing is found) and how much of it exists.

One of the best-known distribution maps is called a dot map. Each dot represents a certain quantity–for example, 10,000 hogs, 5,000 acres of corn, or 1,000 automobiles. When the mapmaker plots this information on a map, the dot pattern immediately shows which areas produce the most hogs, corn, or autos. The numbers used to plot dot maps are usually official statistics collected by county, state, or federal agencies or by industrial or agricultural organizations.

Above: This dot map shows corn production in the United States. Each dot represents 10,000 acres of corn, so the dot pattern gives an instant picture of how much and where corn is produced. The map was drawn using U.S. government statistics.

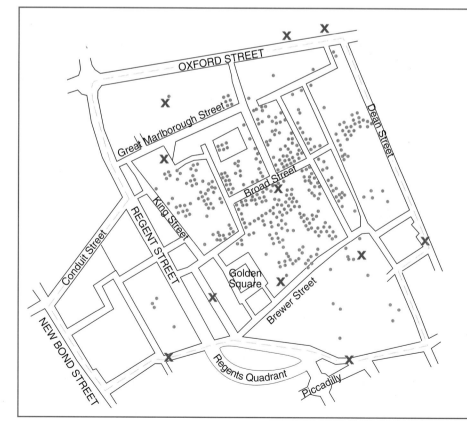

A very famous map

In 1854 London physician Dr. John Snow ended an outbreak of cholera with the aid of a dot map. He plotted each death and also the location of the 11 water pumps in the neighborhood. From the map, Snow saw that the deaths were clustered near the Broad Street pump. He guessed that contaminated water was the cause of the epidemic and had the handle removed from the pump to prevent anyone else using it. No new cases occurred.

X Pump

• Deaths from cholera

– – – Border of survey

Right: This proportional circle map of the main fishing ports in the United Kingdom provides more detailed information than the dot map, but only for a few specific places. You can estimate the tonnage of fish landed at each port by measuring the diameter of the port's circle against the scale at the bottom. [1 metric tonne is just over 2,204 pounds.]

To represent numbers or levels of value, mapmakers can also draw symbols of different sizes. For example, small triangles could signify minor steel-making towns, medium-sized triangles could represent secondary steel centers, and large triangles could symbolize primary steel producers. An alternative is to use symbols whose sizes vary in direct proportion to the numbers they represent. These **proportional maps** supply more information because each symbol stands for an actual number instead of a broad category. Mapmakers use proportional circles to indicate city populations and proportional arrows to show imports and exports.

Another way cartographers can provide information is to divide the numbers into a series of categories with each category shown in a different color or tone and each one covering a range of values. This method could be applied to maps of annual rainfall, population density (the number of people per square mile), life expectancy (how long people live), and income (how much the average person earns).

Pies, Bars, and Graphs

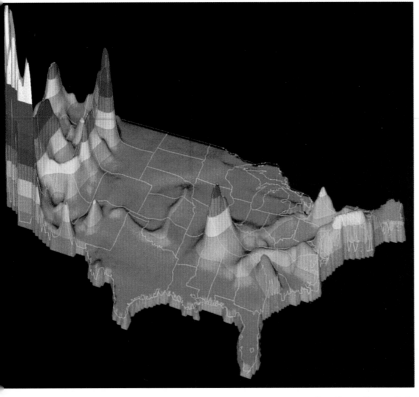

Above: Computers can generate dramatic and instantly understandable graphics from masses of figures. This one shows the risk of an area being hit by an earthquake. Not surprisingly, the San Andreas fault system in California–which marks the boundary of two moving sections of the earth's crust–shows up as the country's highest-risk area.

Right: The pie diagrams on this map provide a summary of European tourism at a glance. The diameter of each pie indicates the total number of tourists, while the segments show where they come from, as a percentage of the total.

Some statistics are too complicated to show simply by dots or colors, so thematic cartographers have invented other ways of handling this kind of information. They use pie charts, bar charts, and other **graphics** to display the numbers in a way that can be understood quickly and easily. A single graphic placed near the center of each region on a map will provide a summary of the information for that region. These days computer software makes it easy to convert figures into graphics at the touch of a few keys.

Mapmakers often draw pies or bars to show both a total amount and how that total is split into various components. For example, the size of the pie chart could represent all the farmland in a state, while the pie's segments could indicate how much of the total is devoted to the raising of grain crops, vegetables, fruits, hogs, cattle, sheep, and dairy products.

Total number of tourists

40,000,000
25,000,000
10,000,000
5,000,000

Origin of tourists

France	Germany
UK	Spain
Ireland	Italy
Netherlands	USA
Denmark	Others
Belgium	Portugal

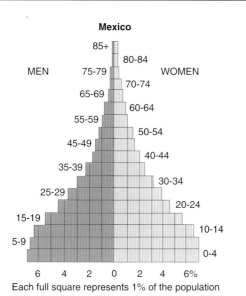

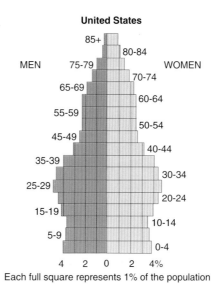

Left: Population pyramids let you compare the populations of different countries. Each layer shows the number of people in that age group. Developing countries have large numbers of young people (high birth rate) but not so many old people (high death rate). Developed countries have far fewer babies but their people live longer. These data produce a much less steeply tapered diagram.

Bar charts can be used in the same way. The bar's overall length represents the total quantity, and the smaller sections show the various components. With bar charts, mapmakers can also compare quantities over a number of years. Instead of dividing the bar into sections, the cartographer draws a separate bar for each year and lines up the bars side by side. You can see at a glance if the totals are increasing or decreasing.

Pies, bars, and other graphics do not contain as much detail as the original statistics, but they quickly summarize the information. They allow a mapmaker to indicate patterns and to compare information. If the information is part of an official document or a scientific report, the statistics are usually listed at the back of the report as a set of **tables**. That way, people can pull from the report various sets of information. The maps and graphics are a convenient summary showing the main patterns and trends, and the tables provide detail for people who want the exact figures for a particular area.

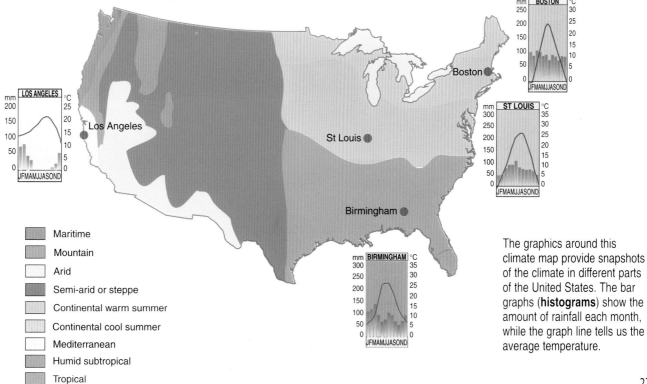

The graphics around this climate map provide snapshots of the climate in different parts of the United States. The bar graphs (**histograms**) show the amount of rainfall each month, while the graph line tells us the average temperature.

27

Time Travel

Where would you be and what would you be doing if half of you was in Tuesday and the other half was in Wednesday? You'd be straddling the International Date Line, which runs down the middle of the Pacific Ocean.

Because of the earth's shape and rotation, one half is lit by the sun while the other half is in darkness. Each point on the earth's surface goes from day to night and back again once every 24 hours. People everywhere set their local time by the sun. Daytime starts when the sun rises. At midday the sun is at its highest point in the sky. Day turns to night as the sun sets. But the earth's rotation means that morning arrives at different times depending on where you live. If you live and work in one place all the time, it doesn't really matter what time it is 5,000 miles away. But if you travel the world on business or make international telephone calls, you do need to know. You want to call your associates during office hours–not in the middle of their night!

So, for convenience, the world is divided into 24 time zones, each of which is one-hour wide. The zones are numbered from the Greenwich Meridian, which is the zero longitude line through Greenwich in London, England. In the time zones lying west (or slow) of Greenwich, local time is earlier than at Greenwich, while local time in the zones east (or fast) of Greenwich is later. Halfway around the world, at 180 degrees longitude, the time on one side of the longitude line is 12 hours earlier than Greenwhich, while the time on the other side of the line is 12 hours later. As you cross the International Date Line, the date changes by one day.

ACTIVITY

Night and Day

You can watch how sunrise and sunset follow each other in your own city by shining a strong light like a flashlight or desk light onto a globe in a darkened room. As you turn the globe slowly from west to east you will see the East Coast cities of North America passing from day into night while the West Coast is still in bright "sunshine." Half a turn later, it is sunrise on the East Coast while the West Coast is still in darkness. After one full turn of the globe, it is nightfall again in the East Coast cities.

Above: On land the lines marking the time zones zigzag around most country borders so that all the clocks in a country show the same time. However, some very big countries like Canada, the United States, and Russia span several time zones. At sea the lines run straight along the north-south longitude lines, except where islands get in the way. Then the lines are bent around the islands to avoid unnecessary time changes. In the same way, the International Date Line zigzags around the islands of the Pacific so that the islands in each group will have the same date.

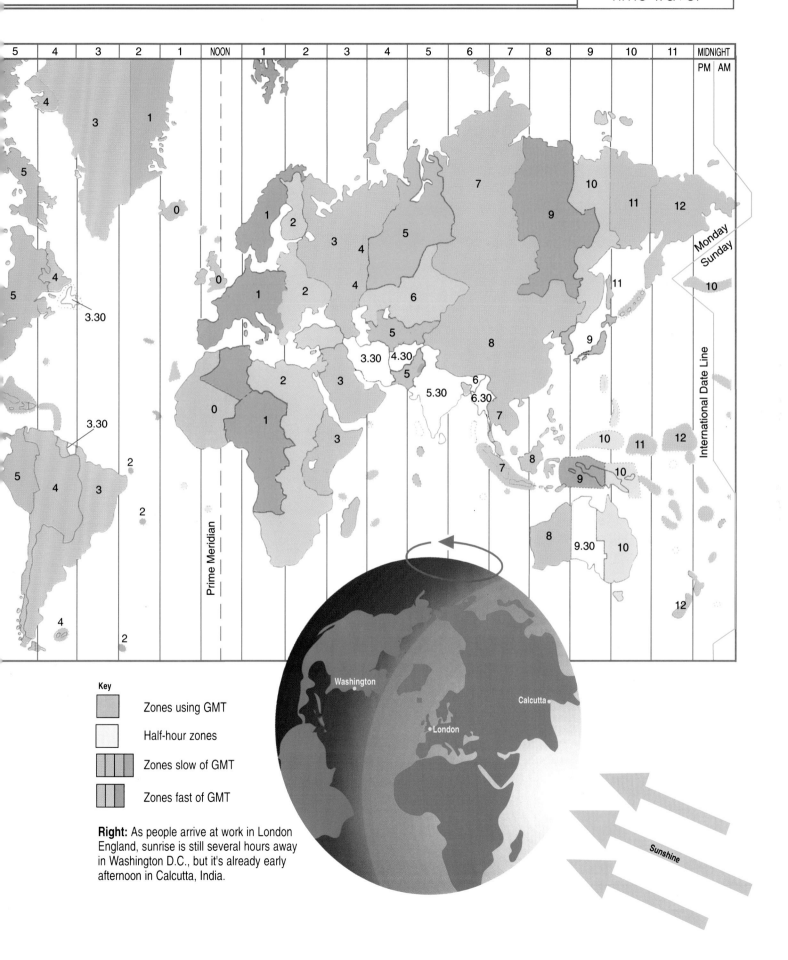

| 5 | 4 | 3 | 2 | 1 | NOON | 1 | 2 | 3 | 4 | 5 | 6 | 7 | 8 | 9 | 10 | 11 | MIDNIGHT |

PM AM

4

3

1

5

0

4

5

4

3.30

3.30

5

4

3

2

2

2

4

2

1

2

0

0

1

2

3

4

5

4

6

5

3.30 4.30

5

5.30

3

3

2

1

7

9

10

11

12

Monday
Sunday

10

11

9

8

6
6.30

7

7

8

8

9

10

10

11

9.30

10

11

12

12

Monday
Sunday

International Date Line

Prime Meridian

Key

Zones using GMT

Half-hour zones

Zones slow of GMT

Zones fast of GMT

Sunshine

Washington

Calcutta

London

Right: As people arrive at work in London England, sunrise is still several hours away in Washington D.C., but it's already early afternoon in Calcutta, India.

You Are Here

These days many of the buildings we visit are so big you need a map to find your way around them. These superbuildings include hospitals, department stores, supermarkets, airports, schools, and museums. Largest of all are shopping malls, which are more like enclosed downtown areas than individual buildings.

The world's biggest shopping mall is the West Edmonton Mall in Alberta, Canada. The mall covers an area of 5.2 million square feet and contains 11 department stores, more than 800 other stores, and more than 100 places to eat. The complex also has a miniature golf course, a water park with wave machines, a dolphin show, nightclubs, movie theaters, an amusement park, a zoo, a 360-room hotel, and parking for 20,000 cars. No wonder you need a map!

The largest mall in the United States is the Mall of America, in Bloomington, Minnesota. The Mall of America has 4.2 million square feet of stores on its 78-acre site and features Camp Snoopy and UnderWater World as its centerpieces.

People who regularly use these superbuildings soon learn their way around them because they eventually remember the layout. For first-time visitors, it's a different matter, but help is at hand. Just inside the entrance to these buildings you will usually find one of the "You Are Here" display boards showing the layout of the building, floor by floor, with all the departments marked. Similar display boards are placed at the top of the elevators and escalators for the benefit of people moving between floors. At very large building complexes, you can usually pick up a visitor's guide containing a map of the entire site, naming all the buildings and showing all the floor plans.

Above: The Mall of America is a huge enclosed shopping and entertainment complex–like a town that has been roofed over. The guide book contains plans of each of the four levels, with color keys and symbols to help visitors find their way around.

Right: Tens of thousands of passengers pass through New York's JFK Airport every day. Ground plans like this one of the main terminal buildings and large signs, many of them with symbols for the benefit of non-English speakers, help people get to their eventual destination.

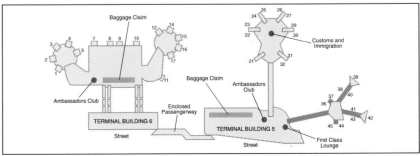

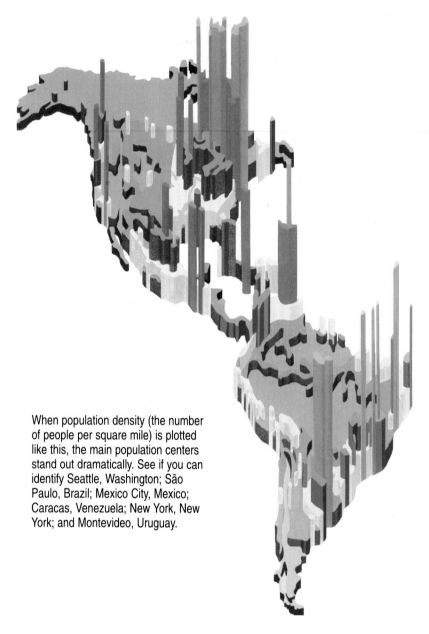

When population density (the number of people per square mile) is plotted like this, the main population centers stand out dramatically. See if you can identify Seattle, Washington; São Paulo, Brazil; Mexico City, Mexico; Caracas, Venezuela; New York, New York; and Montevideo, Uruguay.

Eye-catchers

Most maps have a serious purpose, but that doesn't mean they all have to look alike. Mapmakers sometimes create unusual and strange-looking maps to catch our attention. We stop, look at the map carefully, and think about what the map is saying.

For example, a cartographer may want to make a dramatic statement about the enormous differences in living standards between the rich and poor nations of the world. Instead of using ordinary maps with color keys to show how many people live in each country, or how much food they have to eat, or the value of the goods they produce, the mapmaker lets the map itself tell the story. The designer might redraw the world so that the size of each country is in proportion to the population, amount of food produced, or value of goods.

Maps also help us understand sizes and distances. For example, comparing the size of the United States to the size of Europe is difficult if you only consider the number of square miles each land area covers. However, if a mapmaker draws the United States on top of a map of Europe, you can easily compare the two. Mapmakers often use this method to show the size of a country or region that is far away and unfamiliar.

Three-dimensional views of the world can also be very eye-catching. Some 3-D maps work like bar graphs, with each country being stretched upward to represent a certain quantity. Mapmakers draw other 3-D maps to look like globes and to show global patterns such as air routes, international communications networks, or the astonishing migrations of birds.

Maps even find their way into company logos and advertising campaigns. Images of the earth from space, photographed by day and by night, provide views of the earth that you can enjoy simply for their own beauty.

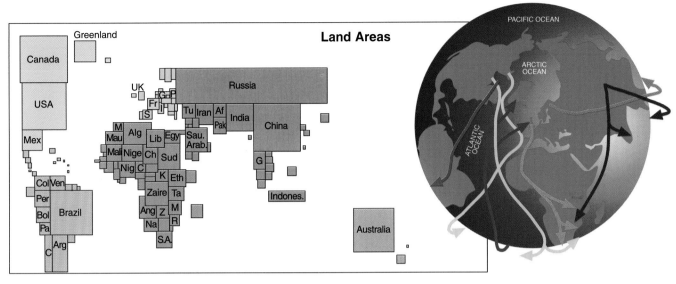

Land Areas

Greenland
Canada
USA
Mex
UK
Fr
S
G P
Russia
Tu Iran
Af
Pak India
China
M
Mau Alg
Lib Egy
Sau. Arab.
Mali Nige Ch Sud
Nig C
K
Eth
Col Ven
Zaire Ta
Per
Ang Z M
Bol Brazil
Na R
Pa
S.A.
C Arg
G
Indones.
Australia

PACIFIC OCEAN
ARCTIC OCEAN
ATLANTIC OCEAN

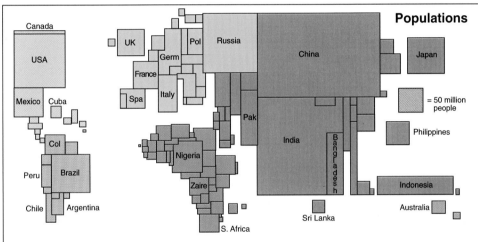

Populations

Canada
USA
UK
Pol Russia
Germ
China
Japan
France
Spa Italy
Mexico Cuba
Pak
= 50 million people
Col
India
Bangladesh
Philippines
Nigeria
Peru Brazil
Zaire
Indonesia
Chile Argentina
Australia
Sri Lanka
S. Africa

Golden Plover
Arctic Tern
Great Shearwater
Swallow
Arctic Warbler
Lesser Cuckoo

Above: Ribbons of color wrapped around a globe are a dramatic way of showing the amazing feats of migrating birds. The Arctic Tern, for example, breeds in the High Arctic but spends the winter in the Southern Ocean on the edge of the Antarctic pack ice.

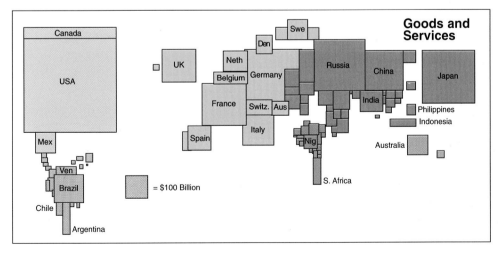

Goods and Services

Canada
Swe
Den
USA
UK
Neth
Russia China
Belgium Germany
India
France
Japan
Switz. Aus
Mex
Italy
Philippines
Spain
Indonesia
Ven
Nig
Australia
Brazil
= $100 Billion
Chile
S. Africa
Argentina

These maps show the world with the countries sized according to their true land areas, their populations, and the value of the goods and services they produce (called the Gross Domestic Product, or GDP). China and India are huge when drawn in proportion to their populations. Australia, on the other hand, appears small. The United States, Japan, and western Europe dominate the GDP map, while Africa, India, and South America, the world's poorest regions, shrink almost out of sight.

Subway, Bus, and Rail Maps

Maps of subway, bus, and railroad routes are unlike most other kinds of maps. The most obvious difference is that many of these maps make no attempt to represent the true distances, scales, directions, or locations of places in the real world. In many ways, these maps are more like diagrams. And with good reason. Mapmakers design route maps to include only the essentials. For subway, bus, or train riders, the essentials are route names or numbers, the order of the stations along each route, and the location of transfer areas where passengers can change routes. All travelers want to know is that they are on the correct route and going in the right direction.

The clearest way to convey this information is to ignore geography. Inner-city routes might twist and turn through the streets or underneath them, while intercity routes wind through the suburbs and beyond. To create easy-to-read maps, however, mapmakers draw the routes as a series of straight lines and rectangular loops.

Actual city bus stops and stations are usually closer together than those in the suburbs. On the route map, cartographers will often ignore these true distances, spacing the stations so that the passengers can easily follow them.

These days bus, railroad, and subway companies utilize these diagram-style maps. The original idea dates to 1931 when Henry Beck, a part-time drafter with the London Underground, designed a new map of the London subway. Inspired by the neatness and clarity of electrical circuit diagrams, Beck created a map of the entire system that was simple, clear, and easy to use. His map is regarded as a classic piece of graphic design.

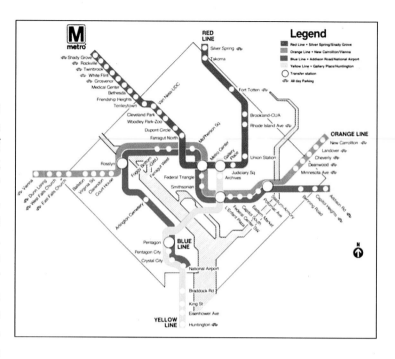

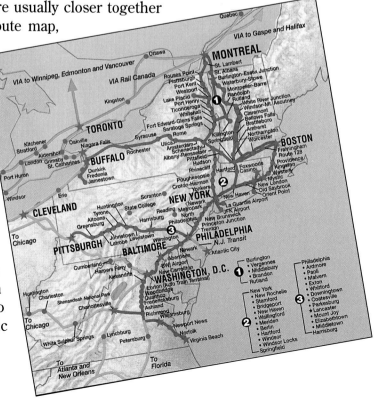

Above: The map of the Washington D.C. Metro is a typical, modern, graphics-style map. Color-coded routes and clear station symbols make the map easy to use. The Amtrak Northeast Area map **(below)** covers a much larger area, and routes are shown in relation to the local geography.

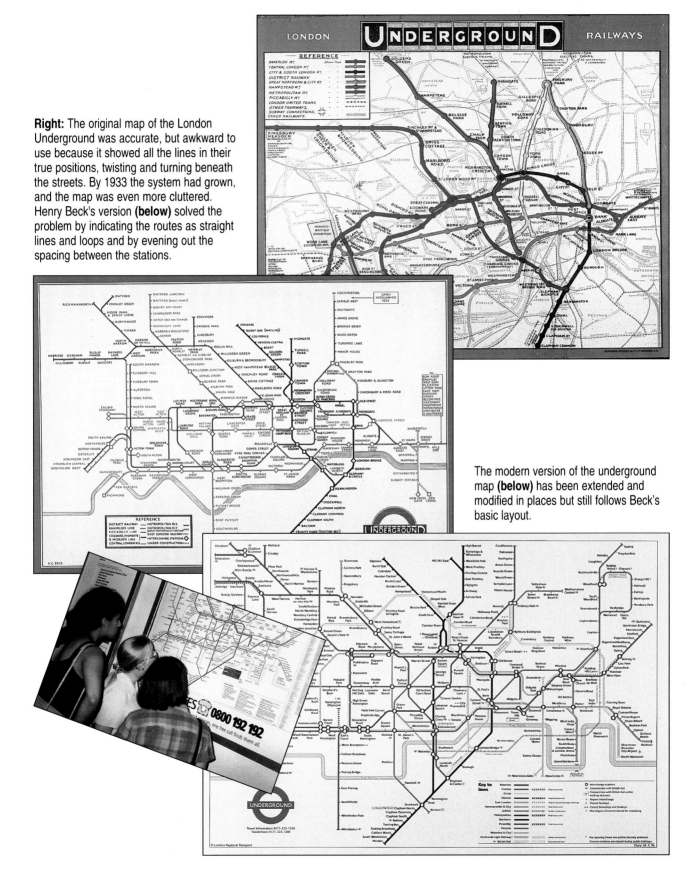

Right: The original map of the London Underground was accurate, but awkward to use because it showed all the lines in their true positions, twisting and turning beneath the streets. By 1933 the system had grown, and the map was even more cluttered. Henry Beck's version **(below)** solved the problem by indicating the routes as straight lines and loops and by evening out the spacing between the stations.

The modern version of the underground map **(below)** has been extended and modified in places but still follows Beck's basic layout.

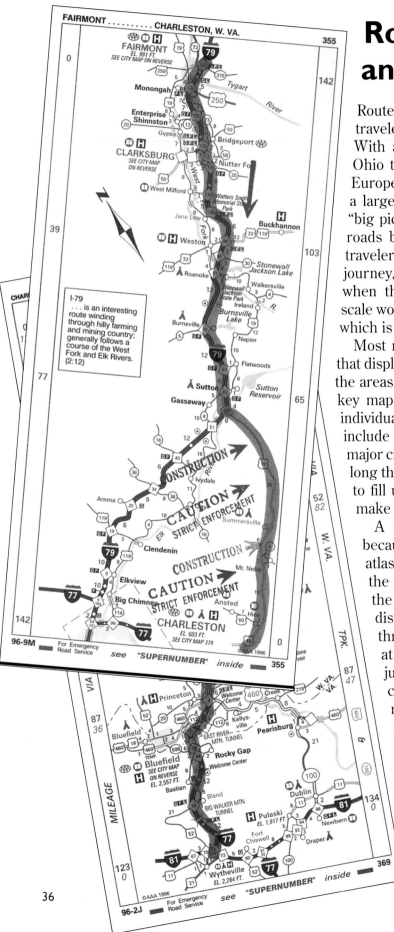

Route Planners and Strip Maps

Route-planning maps are specially designed to help travelers choose the easiest route for a long journey. With a route map, you could plan a journey from Ohio to Oregon or you could plan a car trip across Europe. Route planners are small-scale maps showing a large area but not in much detail. They provide a "big picture" of toll roads, freeways, and other major roads but not of minor roads or small towns. Most travelers use a route planner for the main part of the journey, then change to a more detailed, local map when they get near their destination. A convenient scale would be 1 inch to 1 mile (also written as 1:63,360, which is 1 inch to 63,360 inches–or 1 mile).

Most road atlases provide a key map near the front that displays the entire country, main road networks, and the areas covered by the other maps in the atlas. With a key map, you can select a route and then turn to the individual maps for more detail. Many road atlases also include a mileage chart giving the distances between major cities. These charts are useful for estimating how long the journey will take, how many times you'll need to fill up with gas, and whether or not you'll need to make an overnight stop along the way.

A **strip map** is another useful journey map because it saves you from having to handle awkward atlases or fold-out maps. The strip map shows only the route you have selected. A mapmaker draws the route as a straight line noting intersections, the distances between them, and the towns you'll go through. The map is like a checklist. You can see at a glance where you are, how far it is to the next junction, and where you need to turn off. Auto clubs publish strip maps for the most popular routes, but many travelers create their own, adding notes about favorite rest stops and places to eat.

These strip maps are produced by the American Automobile Association (AAA). Each set of maps covers one specific journey, with the main route highlighted and all the junctions and side roads marked. The maps are stamped with information on road repair and construction work, which may cause delays, and warnings where particularly strict speed limits are being enforced.

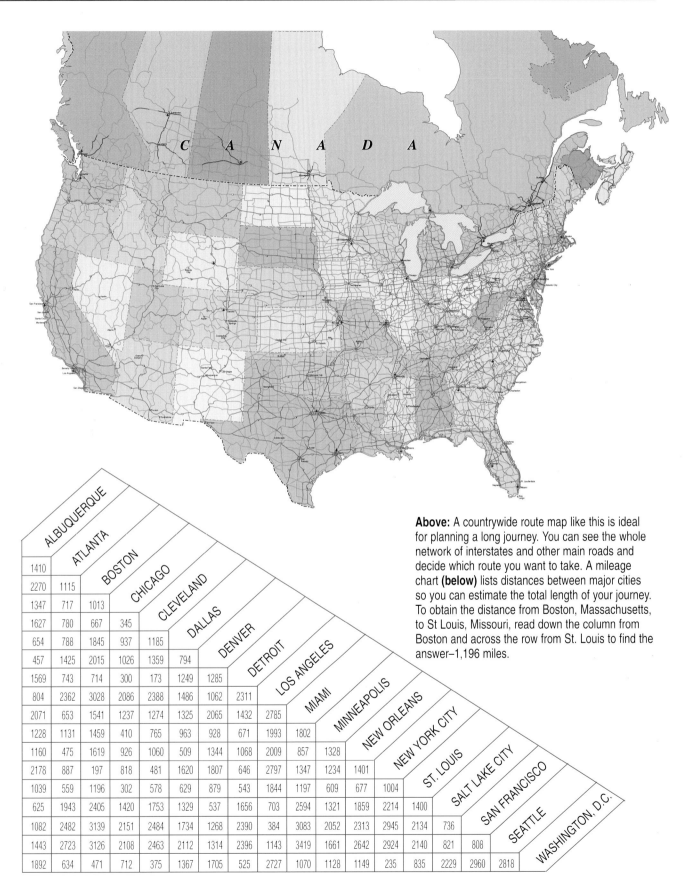

ALBUQUERQUE	ATLANTA	BOSTON	CHICAGO	CLEVELAND	DALLAS	DENVER	DETROIT	LOS ANGELES	MIAMI	MINNEAPOLIS	NEW ORLEANS	NEW YORK CITY	ST. LOUIS	SALT LAKE CITY	SAN FRANCISCO	SEATTLE	WASHINGTON, D.C.
1410																	
2270	1115																
1347	717	1013															
1627	780	667	345														
654	788	1845	937	1185													
457	1425	2015	1026	1359	794												
1569	743	714	300	173	1249	1285											
804	2362	3028	2086	2388	1486	1062	2311										
2071	653	1541	1237	1274	1325	2065	1432	2785									
1228	1131	1459	410	765	963	928	671	1993	1802								
1160	475	1619	926	1060	509	1344	1068	2009	857	1328							
2178	887	197	818	481	1620	1807	646	2797	1347	1234	1401						
1039	559	1196	302	578	629	879	543	1844	1197	609	677	1004					
625	1943	2405	1420	1753	1329	537	1656	703	2594	1321	1859	2214	1400				
1082	2482	3139	2151	2484	1734	1268	2390	384	3083	2052	2313	2945	2134	736			
1443	2723	3126	2108	2463	2112	1314	2396	1143	3419	1661	2642	2924	2140	821	808		
1892	634	471	712	375	1367	1705	525	2727	1070	1128	1149	235	835	2229	2960	2818	

Above: A countrywide route map like this is ideal for planning a long journey. You can see the whole network of interstates and other main roads and decide which route you want to take. A mileage chart **(below)** lists distances between major cities so you can estimate the total length of your journey. To obtain the distance from Boston, Massachusetts, to St Louis, Missouri, read down the column from Boston and across the row from St. Louis to find the answer–1,196 miles.

Picture Maps

Mapmakers can have some fun when drawing picture maps, which often depict popular tourist attractions. Using small illustrations instead of symbols, these maps provide practical information in a clear and easy-to-use manner that is also lively, colorful, and entertaining.

Picture maps help visitors find their way around parks, zoos, nature reserves, ski resorts, and mountain-bike trails. Amusement parks–with their spectacular rides, side shows, playgrounds, picnic areas, mini-farms, and other attractions–often have the most colorful picture maps with the zaniest symbols. Mapmakers might indicate places to eat with a juicy burger or a lip-smacking cartoon figure with knife and fork in hand. A cartoon character diving into a pool full of alligators could represent a swimming area. And people flying out of their seats or hanging on by their fingertips could denote a "white-knuckle" ride.

Even maps of historic towns or battlefields can be presented in an interesting way. Using small illustrations, cartographers can provide an entertaining view of the past–how people dressed, what tools and machines they used, what their transportation options were, and which weapons they used.

Because picture maps present a casual look, you might think they are just rough sketches. But picture mapmakers must first compile an accurate base map with all the features in the correct places. Only then can the cartoon mountains, rivers, buildings, and people be drawn on top.

Below right: Ski resort maps show the roads and villages in the valley and all the cable-cars, chair lifts, and ski tows on the ski areas. The downhill runs are color coded by difficulty–green for the beginners' slopes, then blue, red, and black for the steepest.

Above: This picture map of the Lone Pine resort in California has been drawn as if you were looking down from a mountaintop. The whole layout of the resort, with its main buildings, recreational areas, airport, and access roads, is on view. The map also shows how the resort relates to the valley it is set in, the local hills, and the spectacular mountains around it.

Right: A bird's-eye view reveals Camp Snoopy in the Mall of America in Bloomington, Minnesota. Each feature is in its correct position, but the artist has drawn each one as though it is viewed from a balloon. How many of the rides, theaters, and other attractions can you find?

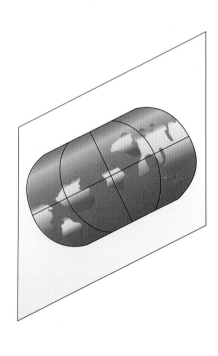

Animated Maps

Most maps are printed–in books, on large flat sheets of paper, on posters, and on display boards. But maps can move as well. The television and computer age allows us to use **animated maps**–maps that move and change.

The first animated maps presented on television were created like cartoon films. Mapmakers drew the map many times on transparent sheets, with the moving part (for example, an army) in a slightly different position each time. Camera operators then photographed the transparencies, frame by frame, so that when the film ran at normal speed, the army appeared to march across the map. These days advanced computer graphics programs allow cartographers to create much more complex moving sequences quickly and economically.

Television weather forecasters rely on animated maps to show hurricanes approaching the coast or weather systems sweeping across the country. News reports from war zones often include animated maps of battle formations and the movements of troops, ships, and aircraft.

Below: Animated maps can reveal how the continents have moved over the surface of the earth during the past. The maps often accompany animated diagrams, which explain the geological processes that make the continents move.

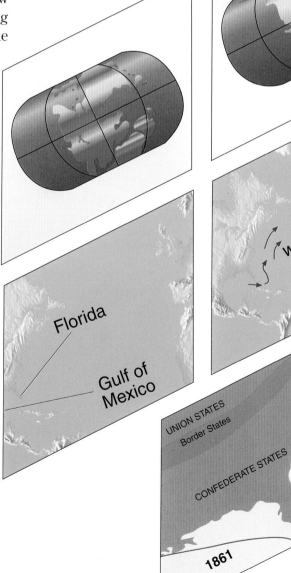

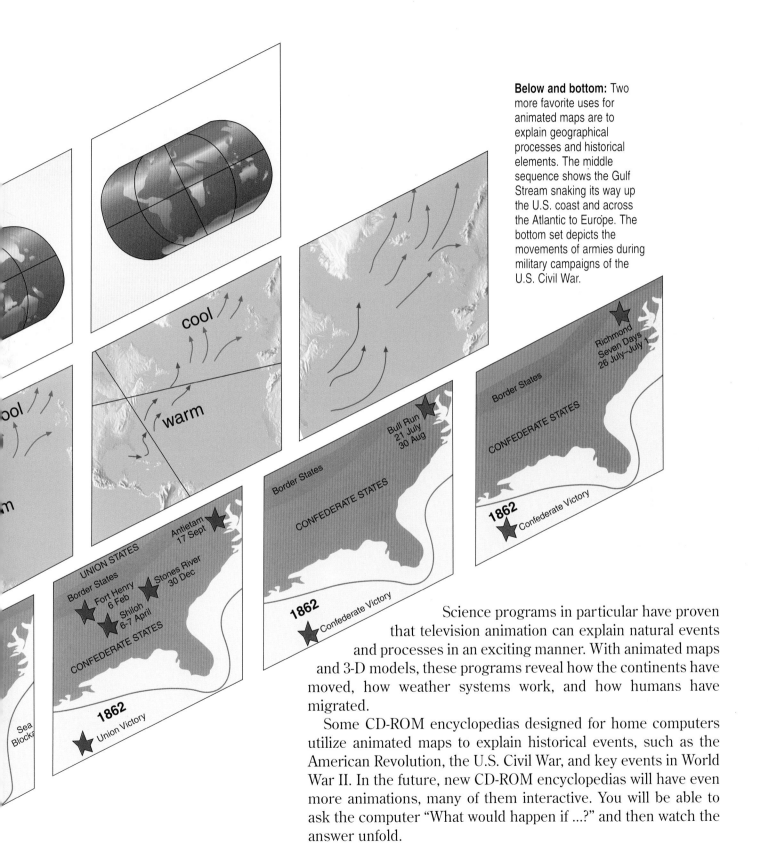

Below and bottom: Two more favorite uses for animated maps are to explain geographical processes and historical elements. The middle sequence shows the Gulf Stream snaking its way up the U.S. coast and across the Atlantic to Europe. The bottom set depicts the movements of armies during military campaigns of the U.S. Civil War.

Science programs in particular have proven that television animation can explain natural events and processes in an exciting manner. With animated maps and 3-D models, these programs reveal how the continents have moved, how weather systems work, and how humans have migrated.

Some CD-ROM encyclopedias designed for home computers utilize animated maps to explain historical events, such as the American Revolution, the U.S. Civil War, and key events in World War II. In the future, new CD-ROM encyclopedias will have even more animations, many of them interactive. You will be able to ask the computer "What would happen if ...?" and then watch the answer unfold.

Maps on Screen

Truckers, company representatives, and other businesspeople who spend a lot of their time traveling around the country have a fast and efficient new way of planning their journeys. Instead of spending time poring over printed road maps, they can do the entire job in a fraction of the time on a computer. With one of the new route-planner software packages loaded onto a PC, all the traveler has to do is enter the starting point and the destination. Within seconds the computer will figure out the quickest route and display it on the screen. The computer will even print out a set of instructions for the journey, telling the driver which route number to leave town on, where to turn off onto a new road, and how long to stay on that road before making the next route change.

A whole road atlas can be stored on a single compact disk, and some software systems can offer several alternative routes. Instead of asking for the quickest route, you can ask for the shortest route, for a scenic route, or for a route that avoids city centers. If you want to plan a touring vacation instead of a journey

Electronic Gateway to America
The Expedia™ Trip Planner 98, launched in 1997 by Microsoft® is a sophisticated computerized journey planner. The CD-ROM database contains the latest maps, covering more than 6 million miles of U.S. roads and 150,000 towns and cities. At the touch of a few keys, the whole country is available on screen.

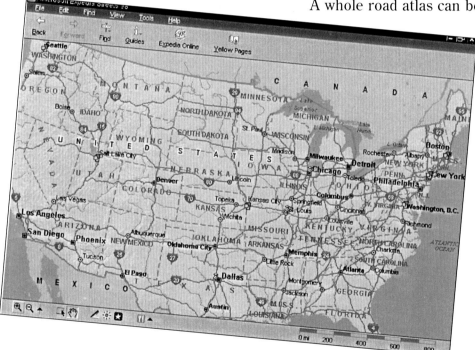

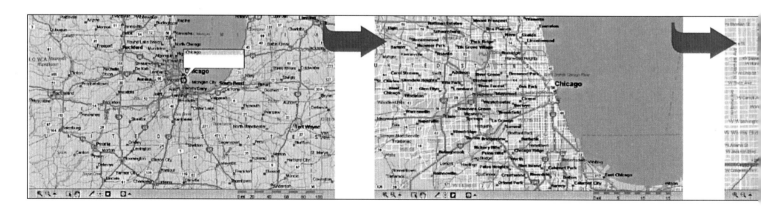

straight from A to B, you can simply browse around the map. A mouse or keyboard controls help you to switch between the map of the whole country and blow-up maps of particular areas. The best electronic map packages even include **gazetteers** (descriptions of places of interest, with opening times and other useful information) so you can plan an entire trip and store it in the computer's memory. When you are satisfied with the tour, you can print out the directions for the whole trip, and you're ready to go.

Computerized street maps are already used in many countries to help police, firefighters, ambu-lance crews, and other emergency services get to accidents quickly. Advanced software is being developed that will be updated constantly with details of traffic conditions, road works, and even faulty traffic lights. The new systems will immediately suggest the best alter-native route for a fire truck or ambulance even if the usual route is blocked by a broken-down vehicle, a fallen tree, or a street parade.

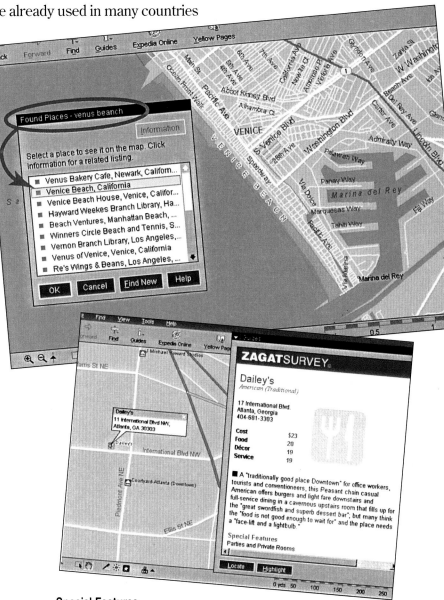

Zoom and Pan
Electronic maps can be resized almost instantaneously. You can view a large area then zoom in to look in closer detail at a smaller area such as a city center or a lakeside resort. If you want to explore the surrounding area, a few simple instructions will pan up or down, left or right, across the map.

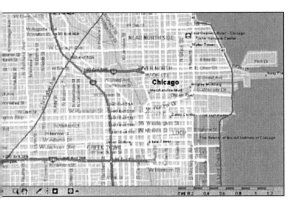

Special Features
Like most of the latest on-screen atlases, Expedia™ contains a quick reference facility. If you know only part of an address, type it in and the computer will find it —even if you make a spelling mistake! And if you need a hotel or a place to eat, you can browse through the listings in the "Where to" guide. With an internet connection, you can even make your reservations on line.

In-Car Maps

Although these days most motorists still plan their trips using road atlases and street maps, some travelers use in-car satellite navigation systems to guide them. After these systems become commonplace, maps will no longer clutter the front seat. They will be stored electronically in the car's navigation computer. A driver will enter the destination using a simple keypad, and in return the computer will display specific route information on a small color screen mounted on the instrument panel and back up this information with spoken directions from a voice synthesizer. (If the driver misses a turning, the computer doesn't get mad or complain. It just calculates a new route.)

The Oldsmobile company led the way in the United States with its Guidestar navigation and information system. Similar systems are being developed across much of Europe. The main components of these systems are an on-board computer, neatly hidden in the trunk; a software package containing the atlas database and operating instructions; a global positioning system (GPS) antenna, mounted on the backseat shelf; and a display screen and keypad that sits in front of the driver.

In the not-too-distant future, your travel plans may take on the following scenario. Before you set off, the computer fixes the car's starting position using signals from navigation satellites. As you proceed, the computer tracks the car's location by constantly monitoring the vehicle's speed (taking information from sensors that monitor how fast the wheels are turning) and the direction in which the vehicle is traveling (from a specialized, in-car compass). From this information, the computer plots the car's position on the map, noting posted speed limits and lane suggestions so you don't miss your exit.

After you have an in-car computer it'll be easy to add extra features. Most of these systems will also include gazetteers and local information about hotels, gas stations, and emergency services–all at the touch of a button. Now that really is progress!

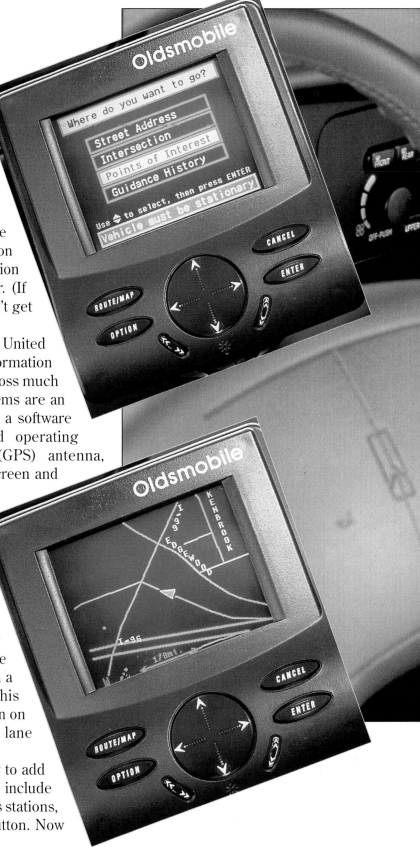

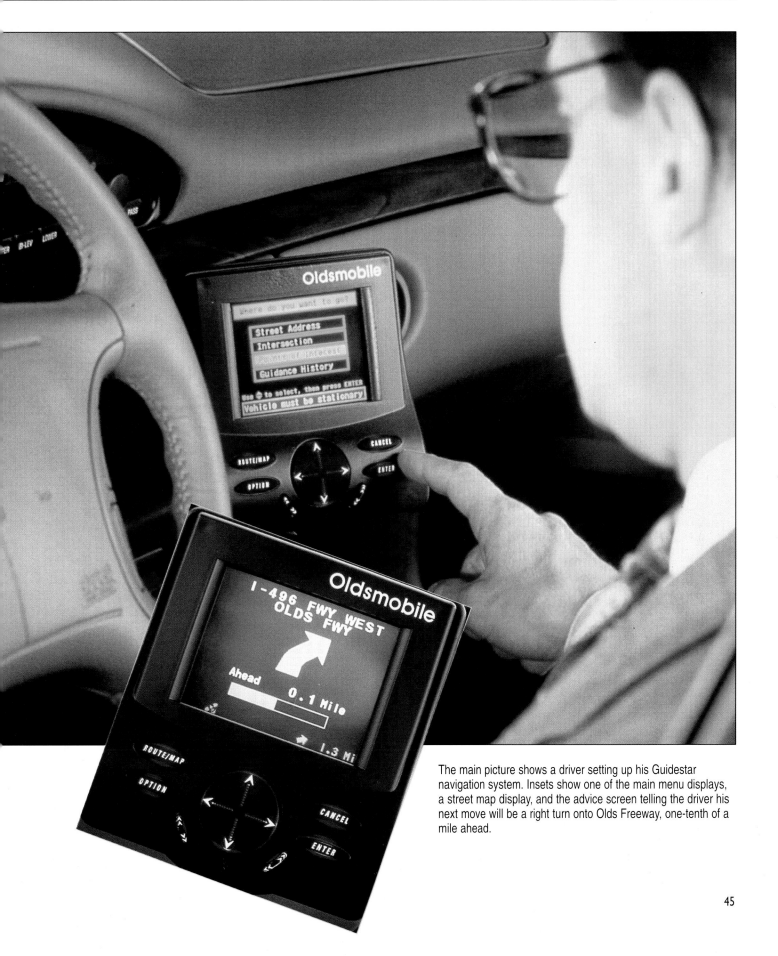

The main picture shows a driver setting up his Guidestar navigation system. Insets show one of the main menu displays, a street map display, and the advice screen telling the driver his next move will be a right turn onto Olds Freeway, one-tenth of a mile ahead.

Glossary

animated map: Any map that shows information in motion–such as weather systems moving across the country or troop movements in a war report. Such maps are viewed on TV or on computer screens.

atlas: A book containing maps. There are several different types. General atlases show countries, landforms, climate, and vegetation. Motorist atlases plot roads and towns. Economic atlases contain maps of food production, industrial output, energy resources, trade, and financial information.

clinometer: A small instrument for measuring the slope of a layer of rock. Geologists call this angle of slope the "dip" of the rock layer.

compiler: The person who decides exactly what information will be on a map and then gathers it together so it can be plotted on the base map.

contour line: A line on a map joining places that are exactly the same height above sea level. Imagine if you poked you knee above the water level in the bathtub, and drew a line around it at water level. Then raised your knee slightly higher and drew another line, and so on. The lines would be contour lines.

gazetteer: A kind of geographical dictionary, containing a list of places along with other details. For towns, information would include where the town is located, how many people live there, what its main activities are (e.g. farming, manufacturing). For museums, the list would include opening times, telephone number, and how best to get there.

graphic: A symbol, graph, or other visual device that is used to portray information.

histogram: A graphic device consisting of bars or columns whose length represents a particular quantity (number of people, tons of steel, amount of rainfall in a month, etc).

igneous rocks: Rocks formed from molten magma deep beneath the earth's surface.

key: A list of the colors, line thicknesses, and symbols used on a map, with explanations of what they stand for.

metamorphic rocks: Rocks that have been altered by extreme heat and pressure, for example in mountain-building processes. The rocks might originally have been either igneous or sedimentary rocks.

meteorologist: A scientist who specializes in the study of weather systems and in predicting (forecasting) what the weather will do next.

proportional map: A map in which the size of a symbol is used to carry information about a particular quantity.

scale: The number of miles (or kilometers) of the earth's surface that are represented by each inch (or centimeter) on the map.

sedimentary rocks: Rocks such as sandstone and limestone that are made from worn-down fragments of older rocks.

strip map: A narrow map in which only the user's main route is shown, with details of junctions, distances between checkpoints, and so on.

table: A list of numbers (also called data), such as trade figures, climate statistics, population details, etc.

thematic map: A map showing just one particular type of information (one topic, or theme), such as climate, geology, or land use.

topographical map: A map showing the shape of the ground. Also called a relief map or a physical map.

vegetation map: One of the most common thematic maps. The map usually shows the natural vegetation that would cover the land if no forests had been cut down, no marshes had been drained, and no grasslands or woodlands had been plowed to make way for crops or livestock.